BUILDING INTO AIR

LAWRENCE SAIL

Building into Air

BLOODAXE BOOKS

ISBN: 1 85224 335 X

First published 1995 by
Bloodaxe Books Ltd,
P.O. Box 1SN,
Newcastle upon Tyne NE99 1SN.

Bloodaxe Books Ltd acknowledges
the financial assistance of Northern Arts.

Cover printing by J. Thomson Colour Printers Ltd, Glasgow.

Printed in Great Britain by
Cromwell Press Ltd, Broughton Gifford, Melksham, Wiltshire.

for Helen

Acknowledgements

Acknowledgements are due to the editors of the following publications in which some of these poems first appeared: *Critical Survey*, *New Statesman & Society*, *PN Review*, *Poetry Review*, *Poetry Review India* and *The Spectator*. 'The Sitting-Room' was first published in *Poems for Alan Hancox* (The Whittington Press, 1993).

The epigraphs for the book's opening section are taken from W.H. Auden's *Collected Shorter Poems 1927-1957* (Faber, 1966), Kenneth White's *The Bird Path* (Penguin, 1990) and Robert Jungk's *Children of the Ashes* (Penguin, 1963).

Lawrence Sail wishes to thank the Arts Council of England for a Writer's Bursary awarded in 1993.

Contents

1

Three cities
would take several tellings
I laugh to myself

KENNETH WHITE,
Haiku of the Sud-Express

Across the square
Between the burnt-out Law Courts and Police Headquarters
Past the Cathedral far too damaged to repair,
Around the Grand Hotel patched up to hold reporters,
    Near huts of some Emergency Committee,
    The barbed wire runs through the abolished City.

W.H. AUDEN,
Memorial for the City

... that naked, hairless and eyeless horse that so many of
the survivors claimed to have seen in the ruined streets of
Hiroshima during the first days after the disaster. Its long
skull was encrusted with blood, for it was continually col-
liding with the few walls and ruined houses that were still
standing; it would stumble on, wandering to the irregular
rhythm of its hoofbeats, now with flaring, puffing nostrils,
now with sunken head, now walking, now mournfully trot-
ting; on and on through the city as it searched for a stable
that was no longer there...

ROBERT JUNGK,
Children of the Ashes

Sketch

The city, which calls to mind
its own ignorance, its distance
from the waterfall that pours
over the lip of the hanging valley,
from the valley meadows packed with flowers,
from the great impervious beauty
of the high water cascading,
and the flowers that, countless, die.

Such will to order,
such unnatural power,
the night lit all through.

The Expedition

1

Early on, we dreamed
That we no longer had
A proper language, that
The punctuation had lost
All sense of order –
A breaker's yard
Of brackets, towering
Exclamations,
Stops running out
Into rank water...

2

When we turned away
To climb to the hinterland,
We could still hear
The inroading sea,
Its long scroll
Unfurling across
The glittering mica.
We listened to it almost
For longer than possible.

3

Basketwork, rafia
Bags or mats,
Oil-tins bent
Into mugs with handles,
Rabbits held out
In upturned hats,
Grubby salt-licks,
At night the sporadic
Kingdom of paraffin:
All of this
Was comprehensible.

4

Miles beyond
The backland's columns
Of jointed basalt,
Its wild escarpments
And cloud-choked forests,
There was said to be
Some crazed perfection
Of a capital, complete
With ten-lane boulevards,
Buildings as wide
As the open sea,
A bicycle to every
Thousand citizens.

5

One day we talked
Of home – the towns
Where shadow was perpetual,
With their little moon clocks,
Reliable markets
And the crackle of coal
In bellied iron grates.

6

Even the new coast
Has become articulate
In remembrance – the falling
Land clipped by salt
To the neatness of topiary;
The dusty square,
Its stoppered cannon
Thick with lacquer
And the stringy flagpole
Always ready
To salute a régime.

7

Almost the last
Words of our leader
Had to be heard
In the absurd context
Of whooping birds,
The gibber of monkeys,
The clicks and whistles
Of God knows what.
We have no authority,
He said – and the language
Simply came apart.

8

Tomorrow we press forward
To found a nation.

Before the Founding of the City

1

Bring pegs so as to mark out the place.
Bring two crowbars so as to dig post-holes.
There are no crowbars? All right then, sharpen two sticks.
Send out two men to the forest to cut forked pillars,
Two to look for strips of bark, and two more
To cut grass and others to look for posts.

2

The baboons have eaten all the peas and beans.
The clerk's daughter wants to buy some beads.
You have not yet paid your tax, what tribe are you?
If you want leave to be circumcised, I will sign
The registration certificate that you require.
All right, give me twenty-five cents, and I will give you
A stamp, some paper and an envelope.

3

Certain machines are distinguished by the sound they make.
Have you enough petrol to start the coffee pulper?
Is there any sim-sim oil for the thongs of the whips?
I shall plant fig trees to shade the coffee bushes.
The sun is strong, the stones are exceedingly hot.
The train has arrived. The almond trees are in fruit.
Bring me my photographs and that yard measure.
Tomorrow we build. I will write out your agreement.

(with acknowledgement to *Up-Country Swahili* 'for the soldier, settler, miner, merchant, and their wives: and for all who deal with up-country natives without interpreters': F. H. Le Breton, first edition 1936)

First City

In the first city I learn
the meaning of street level:
in the shadow of three faiths,
the shared belief in padlocks,
hasps, grilles, mesh,
nailed chipboard, iron bars.
And somewhere there is a window
locked solid with paper.

In the empty public gardens
the security men are talking
on their radios. Their bunches of keys,
heavy as a bull's balls,
weigh importance.

Beyond the undissenting suburbs
where the dentists surely live,
there is a road that goes on
for ever, where men in parked cars
are making anxious deals,
or failing to get in touch
with home on their mobile phones.

How the golden dome of the mosque
burnishes the sunlight to new!
And in the same sunlight,
near Limehouse Lock, a boy
and a girl are sliding through
a gap in the schedule of railings.

And who is that man petrified,
with his stone case to heel, outside
the station? It is hard enough
to live as any hero,
let alone the leader
of an expedition to Loughborough
undertaken for temperance.

Paddy (dear heaven, how he laughs
at the camouflage of his name!)
somehow must get across
three major roads, carrying
his bag of extra strong cider,
to the safety of the Red Cow.
He's OK, but his head
hurts where he was beaten up,
Christ it hurts, but he knows
enough to shake the hand
of whoever helps him get there.

By the main gate of the cemetery
it is all clearly typed out –
the distance the law requires
between bone and brick,
coffin and vault, neighbour
and neighbour, and cold earth.

And how shall the word
ever comprehend the flesh?
The word in acronyms,
the word in Gujarati,
the word in the underpass
where a man and his dog
express a single curse:
the flesh in the tonnage of dust,
the flesh in the piled markets,
the flesh in the growing gaps
that words leave between them.

*Twelve oranges a pound
twelve juicy oranges there a pound
twelve oranges in a carrier bag
twelve juicy oranges in a carrier bag
twelve juicy oranges there in a carrier bag.*

And who is that impresario
of the wholesale hangar, researching
the great cauliflower scam,
his thin mouth barely holding
a fat, cheap cheroot?

City of exquisite addictions,
your sweetshops split
each atom of taste
and confect each shape
to responsible living:
beyond the countless
emporiums of sarees
stitched and studded
a thousand times,
Ganesh looks
completely at home
in the bays of inland villas.

Two Views of the City

The first, optically false but true – the vertical,
the image of the thematic mapper sensor –
dear God, you think, and how could anyone live
in such a vascular wilderness, when the river
is already more black than blue, and seems to cringe
away from the land? And then, the land itself,
dyed into patterns of heat and bruised blue...

The second, horizontal – you squint across the roofs
to more walls and more roofs, and then more walls –
but everywhere, the windows march along
and up and down, sucking the poor day in.
The sunlight that strikes the occasional blank surface
is the last. If you wanted a proof of madness, you know
it is here, in the angles which finally cannot hold.

Second City

Someone must have read it
as a threat – the weight of civic pride,
the stupendous mass
of a reclining woman,
the four great stone lions
eroding to a sick pallor.

It is said that the moon
is never seen above this city,
and that each night a voice
proclaims the death of the lyric
in its dreamless streets: and, yes,
above the patchy darkness
diluted by orange,
the stars go by.

And it can seem that simple
when by ten at night
the deserted streets are dug
and drilled under arc-lights –
or at noon, when the city
stands back from the river
and all its tatty towers
shrink to perspectives of distance.
Or at any time, throughout the city,
when the brewery's absurd huntsman
begins to raise his glass
but never slakes his thirst.

You look like a gentleman.
I wouldn't be asking you otherwise.
Something for a sandwich.
I spent last night cold
and locked up into the bargain.
They said I was drunk but I wasn't.

The hospital, the library, the courts:
everything bloated, simply just too big,
tripping over itself, like the hillside
that has become an administrative
headquarters, its contours
mashed to tarmac access.

But the camouflage itself fails –
the brand names, the chain stores,
the *décors*, and the outdoor escalators
already bright with moss,
the church tower cobwebbed with cables
for fairy lights, by the flagpole
bandaged in saffron cloth:
even the poet attempting
to sneak past under the cover
of a top hat. Even the man
snapping the wipers off cars.

Everywhere, you suffer the weight
that throbs off the angles and acoustic
of water, that aches up through your feet
as you skirt the uncrossable carriageways;
that presses down through the tower blocks.

What changes hands down the long roads
out of the centre, is one or another
version of the rumoured velocity of escape.
In one palm, money; in another, money.
Between them, the trip, the wad shot. Yeah.

And everywhere, the bright attempt to build
the city's simulacrum into high air,
to roof in the clouds
or suspend a biplane from wires,
to construct terraces that give onto
pure layers, with thoroughfares
of wind and rain, balustrades
for sunlight to lean over.

Would-be arcades of amnesia
full of glitter! But what really shines
is the thought of heavy bulldozers, heaving
the lot – jewellery, crafts, crystal,
aromatic lotions, leather goods, watches,
finest knitwear and fancy breads –
over the edge, into the sea.
In the blue corner, those who believe
in aesthetics and stewardship:
in the red, the champions of
community and conscience.
Let all the world...

Between the clouds and the stone, there is
one green bottle, balanced on a wall,
half light, half full – and this:
the voice of its owner, from across the road,
as he leans into the gutter and wails,
For Chrissake, I'm only forty-seven!
(and the whole of the city seems to lie
refracted in the liquor's
bright, stilled horizontal)
Only forty-seven years of age!

An apparently endless silence,
a time-lapse sequence jammed
at a point where glass
refuses to crumble to sand
or fuse to rock:
and, in the Mandela Gardens,
where the tulips are in their cups,
nothing stirs to confirm or deny
his words locked into stone:
the struggle is my life.

The Authorities Attempt to Keep in Touch

Like, nobody wacks the rulers' tag,
since they are always fly and dope –
it's time to tell you our party's kicking.
This is nothing lame and nothing rank:
we want to be your homies, your crew.
We're no way sketch, our G. style's rad –
don't you go saying we're a ho
or that we're getting busy. Like,
we're O.G., you better check it out,
we're chill on slate, no hole in our bucket,
hot knife or bong or skinning up's
cool on any turf, we're tooled up,
we've got the juice, the decks and rags –
don't you step to us or say we're wiggers
or biscuit heads. We're stupid, the law,
we've got your G. style and your jewels,
we're on a trip and stoked. If you kick
off, we'll soon be painting black tears.
Like, nobody wacks the rulers' tag:
our homies, if you're cool, that's you.

Third City

Somewhere between
the two cathedrals
an unhurried sax
yawns the length
of a whole dark street,
plosive, then
huskily pulsing,
lax and lovable.

It could not be enough
to make for coherence,
though it conjures nostalgia,
the ghost of hope:
here, no gloss of renewal
can quite exorcise
the pale ships that nose
through early mists,
the buried lines,
the fairground rattle
of the airborne railway.

But what is more wrecked
than a stove-in roof?
What grass is tougher
than the roof-level tussocks?
What could be more on fire
than the roaring waste,
the rage of endless torching?
Here, the psalms
are true songs of anger.

At times like this
you would say, perhaps,
that the city was ill-founded
or gone to seed:
too many scumbled stones,
too much paintwork
all scab and crust;

too often exhibiting,
as with the wire
exoskeleton of the palm house,
a pathology beyond reason.
Too many ownerless dogs
that run towards you
at a menacing diagonal,
their large ears pricked up:
too many bottles lobbed
into hopeless areas.

It is nothing that time
cannot also cure.
Meanwhile, in one cathedral
crouches a secret brass mouse,
an antidote for children
to the gaunt scale of belief;
in the other, the archbishop
is pictured showing
a docker's hook
to Monsignor Furneval,
as if to say
that here too
the world is everything
that is the case.

In the mute shadows
of words, in the inches
of their worn columns,
somewhere there is hidden
the exposed life
of the actual city,
where the saxophone leaves
each phrase wide open
to interpretation
and the river's régime
goes on for ever.

Near Endings

Flayed by fire
the horse of Hiroshima
knocks its blind bone and blood
against brick, wood.

On another coast
the rain surges in swathes,
trees flip like tossed cabers,
even though the trams go on
dragging their rust and clank
on from prehistory.

To each city its bunting,
its brightness, its high tides,
its inflorescence of rusts,
its mechanisms of disaster,
the moment when all the little boxes
of livings, the ingenious tins,
are folded away or scattered.

And there comes to each
some laureate of lassitude,
a dark-eyed dandy
of love and war,
or a crusty slippered poet
with his carpetbag spilling
frayed, half-finished maps.
He takes his time,
shambling in the last of sunlight –
commissioned by himself
and pensioned off,
knowing it needs more
than geese to save a city now.
Compline shall be his swansong,
his chosen vanishing-point.

Yet even here,
long after the horse,
after heat that unlocked
the seeds as well as the stones,
the city has fruited
into strange newness –
has gone on to where
the long sickness
begins to look
like just slower forgetfulness,
the brutal inconsequence
of time passing.
Unless those hoofbeats
are not growing fainter
but louder, drumming
our haunted futures.

2

1.30 a.m., twice

And already I remember
The rain in its intensities
As it tuned and varied its volume –
On the first night of the storms,
When the signalling equipment
Blacked out between Exeter
And Plymouth; and the next time,
When somewhere a light aircraft
Overshot the runway.

It all seemed to parade –
The gross stumbling thunder,
The freakish wonders of lightning
That blazed in the drawn curtains;
As if we enjoyed a climate
Completely to ourselves, and lay
At an angle to any time.
I realised then what love
The acoustic of dark could carry.

Your breathing, unsteady, moves
In and out of sleep
Through half broken narratives
That connect dream and fact.
Now and then your long
Slender legs show up
In the pale flashlight. Together
We count the distance of thunder,
The precious seconds of silence.

5 a.m.

At home, it would have been
The milk-float soughing past
With its quivering cargo,
And the first foil-peckers
Starting to sing.

Here, it is the rising bass
Of the early métro as it picks
Up speed and rattles
Beneath the bookshops
Of the Boul Mich.

In France or England, it is you
I have in mind when I wake,
As if to tell me
How simple love is,
How constant its image.

But which days should we lament
More, in the light of dawn –
Those that race by
Or those that grow
Inch by slow inch?

It would be no better to ask
Whether the heart is more expert
At a quick leap
Or the soft ache
Of your absence now.

An Afternoon Walk

Your dog could swim for ever, it seems,
Along and back in the moorland river,
Exploiting his spaniel inheritance
As fluently as a swan.

We sit watching him bite the bubbles
At his own mouth. Above the softly
Buckling water, low cloud
Heats the glare.

As we go back, you throw a simple
Fistful of air for your dog to chase:
He will run for ever, it seems,
Suspending disbelief.

And somewhere in this lies a small quotient
Of sadness, which might be the number of times
That love goes into a lifetime,
Or the plain measure

Of another day played off against
The version of infinity still locked up
In the question I haven't asked
And your answer.

Working Through

We cover the same ground as we did in April –
The path with cows on one side, calves on the other,
The river restless now in the sweat of light,
The green of spring gone over to a blaze
Of near exhaustion: summer overreaching itself.

Where we stretch out, by the water straked with weed,
Each pebble knows how best to knobble our spines.
Overhead, a fighter plane just splinters
The afternoon sky. In the pressure, words might be
Nothing more than a unit of measure for pain.

But we are working through – and still can hold
The surety of silence, its constant dream
Drifting at dusk like a huge harvest moon
That shines and shines on what the heart saves from time.

North to South

Time and again the uncertain distances
Swing between us, veering
Like a mad compass. *Take care,*
You write. *Be strong, be happy.*
But tomorrow, as you head home
On a volatile boat, I shall be
Already skyborne and heading north.

Sometimes it is hardly possible to imagine
That the stars could still be burning
As brightly at noon as at midnight;
Or that any place and time
Might be contained by the heart
In a context free of shadows,
Where the sun and the moon shine together.

But, waking, I recall the tiny crease
By your mouth; the first light
Rounding on your shoulder; the waft
Of your soft breath in the darkness –
And already I am racing south,
Reducing the great generalities
To the small particulars of love.

A Spell Against Parting

Too often it is either, or –
Either the one turning back
To a world gone dull, or even
Sometimes the one who settles
To a book or a fitful sleep
As the aeroplane powers up
Through cloud-drifts into sunlight:
Just one, who seems bereft.

But let it be the two of us
As we come and go, who are kept
Happy by the mad lovely lightning
That welds all the gaps: and who stay
Safe as one, under African heat
Or the drench of the monsoon rain.

In Your Absence

I can offer you only two things,
Whatever their disguises –
One that might be a feather,
It weighs so little, or a hat
Worn at a silly angle, or
A bubble all the colours of petrol:
Whatever is light or funny
Enough to smuggle through customs.

And that other, which cannot mask
Itself, and must be declared –
That quicksilver leap of the heart
Which, like love itself, is suddenly
Naked, a flagrant contraband,
The suitcase gaping under hard lights.

Meeting Again

Before our hands touch, imagine
The air compressed by longing,
The way each step forward
Intensifies the light
Or clarifies the darkness!
It will be something like the spasm
Of cramp that has you jerking
Out of bed as if you had been stung.

After or before our hands touch,
There are always those two figures
Who know what it means to meet
Again as real shadows
In a solvent stillness where
Again and *not yet* become *now*.

Namaskaar

What can these words begin to do,
Folded away and boxed? For you
They ought to be shooting into the sky
As if on springs, or swooping and diving,
Each letter bombarding the room
Like a loose balloon. And the Lodi tombs
Outside should take off in a spurt of flame
And the placid white bullock trample the frame
Of the green Atco it's pulling: and the moon
And stars join the sun in the blaze of noon.

Let the words be. I know that you
Will read between the lines and construe
A subtext of virtual silence, the measure
Of time applying a double pressure:
Those long nights, the endlessly slow defeat
Of darkness – but also the quickening beat
Of the heart. Or let just one word do
For many. *Namaskaar. I bow to you.*
Let this denote the fullness that withstands
The inroads of language. Now, close the box. Take my hands.

Seeing Through Water

Not so much when, on your back
Within the blue-green O of the pool
You lie there, calmly floating,
Open and exposed,
With only the thin lapping sheet
Between you and the sky,

But when you swim length after length
Widely stroking the flow aside,
Is when you seem most at risk,
Most precious – with your hair
Sleekly dark and combed back from your temples
By the water, as you part it.

It is something about the paleness of your brow,
Your head held just clear of the pool
And turned slightly to one side;
Your arms that meet
And spread, pulling the water back,
And close to meet again.

It could be a dream, the way in which
You come and go, crossing the criss-cross
Dimples of blank and blue,
But that the water
Magnifies, clear of all distortion,
A simple, shining truth.

Another Parting

Remember how we gunned the car down the motorway
Towards the airport's absurdly slow
Litanies of departure? – Check-in, the catechism
Of security questions, the electric angelus
Of chimes, passport control, the gate...

When, somehow, we managed to say
Goodbye, we felt we were being crushed
By the weight of time that had massed above us
Like the grey cloud into which you would go:
And, through it all, an orphan half-phrase
Rang in my head – but a mad contradiction
Of what was real – *Time that is given...*
Today, as another parting comes closer,
The words recur, along with that cloud
Which moves over each lived minute of love.

But today those minutes have all the brightness
Of your favourite gemstones – the steady burn
Of garnets, the amethyst's clear purple,
The mallow-green of malachite, with its swirl
Of black contours beneath the surface:
As if parting itself could just be
Like seeing sunlight pinch the ocean
Into points of sparkle, or like the way
In which now that phrase finds its sudden completion –
Time that is given has no shadow.

No shadow – simply the winking grains
Of all those minutes which fire and flare
Along the runways that lead into darkness:
And, beyond, the calm patterns of the stars,
The bearings which fix our new arrivals.

The Bruise

One night you ear-marked me,
Yet even when the bruise blossomed
In mauve and yellow on my arm
Where your head had rested, I failed
To recognise it as
The simple blurred imprint
Of the ear-stud you had worn.

But once you had explained it,
I wore that mark with the pride
Of one on whose poor flesh
Appear the stigmata of a love
Which, even after the cloud
Of old blood has paled,
Still lasts and lasts.

A Walk by Rutland Water

The exactness of the landscape almost dwarfs it –
The way the bathtub steamer rounds the point
Of what is, after all, only a reservoir;
Or the detail of the old Palladian church
Freighted with limestone, that sits on the far shore.

Every little thing performs with absurd precision –
The three fishermen who stand in a line of regression
And cast in turn, fine snake after whistling snake;
The exact ears of the rabbit that twitch into sight
Beside the haybale, and flick away again.

Everything more than real, like the rosy muzzles
Of the bullocks you notice in a field, yet also less,
As we walk together through the sharp autumn light,
Giants of a double vision, made lucky by love.

The Lack of You

Level as any water, constant as clock-time,
The lack of you has occupied the house.
It is an unspent force, a static that fills
The space behind each closed and open door
With the same context. Now, all air contains
The closest memory and the most distant hope
Equally, cancelling neither, and still is empty.

And emptiest of all, the bed in which
We lay last night below the shield of the window,
Where past and future always round to become
Only what touch can tell – the curve of a nail,
The small of your back, the swell of smoothest skin
That falls away: where nothing now but moonlight
Drifts on the buoyant pillow, and time is endless.

Sweet Chestnuts

Not to name the object, but to display
The sweet chestnuts, conceivably becomes
A homage to the simple quiddities –
For instance, how on the drenched October grass
They lie splayed out, their quilled green mace-heads utterly
Exploded to reveal the hair-soft linings
Of not quite yellow, not quite white or grey:
And, oddly square, the tenements of brown fruit,
The three or four that stand up at the centre,
Loosely socketed, easily dislodged.

There comes the sense of something secret shown,
Of some exposure tender to the touch,
An inkling offered of what it is that denies
The object its loneliness, its independence.
Above the fallen fruit, the swelling tree;
Below, the twisting contexts of the roots.
Within the object, unnamed, the hidden subject,
Its absence that homes to you as naturally
As the heart leaps at the single name of its love.

The Earring

This is how you told it – fully
An hour later, it must have been,
That you first missed the light tug of it
At your lobe and, already half despairing,
Retraced your steps into the night
And the blank street drifted with leaves.
In the morning, you knew, a municipal hoover
Would snuffle them and all else away;
Assuming that it hadn't long before
Been kicked out of sight or ground to nothing.

But among the brittle scrap and black shadows,
With the silver setting somehow catching
In the weak field of a streetlight, suddenly
You glimpsed the smoulder of the single garnet.
Amazing luck, we agreed, almost
A miracle – and now in both our minds
Is lodged this little ballad of retrieval
And the sense of loss that it underwrites;
Of which we still know almost nothing, only
That the long odds of love can make it good.

South Street Nocturne

The curtains breathe in and out
To the night wind, and the door
Of the tall cupboard sags open:
It would really be no surprise
If the drawers of the dressing-table
Slid open one by one.

Everything's joining in –
The dressing-gown hunched on its hook,
The louche bedside light,
Its shade pushed back from the heat
At an angle, the alternating hiss
And hiatus of a distant train –

Even the two of us, lying
Beneath the long cord
Of the light-switch that trails
To its plastic toggle; one
Of us asleep, and one,
Apparently, not quite.

Close to the bed, a clock
That seems to slow at each
Flick of a second, as if
None of this could be
(And could it?) more than a set
Piece of indolence, or love.

Ideogram

The way you write the figure 2
Seems purely anecdotal –
A love of narrative overcoming
The simple fact of a total.

You start by sketching a river surface,
A gleaming baseline of ink
That flows from left to right beside
The margin's vertical brink.

Then, rising against the current,
The elegant hook you draw
Is a fine swan's neck, rounding to dip
Down to the water once more.

You do it at speed, as if by sleight
Of hand, but still it displays
A figurative meaning more
Than sense alone conveys:

The sum of love as two-in-one
And more than either one could make –
The whole story of the river rewritten
Victoriously in the swan's wake.

The Valentine Voltage

What we push out is not a trail
Of gently rising Zs – and, although
Shop windows are plumped with scarlet satin,
Not even a glowing tracer burst
Of pulsing hearts, the kind that leave
Micky's Minnie madly blushing,
Hugging herself in a spasm of love.

What we push out is a single X
That sparks and crackles wickedly
For a split blue second, stinging our lips
Quite painfully. It's caused, you say,
By my rubber soles and the build-up of static
In the cover of the chair. Wryly we rub
The prickle of pain away with our fingers.

Perhaps, like me, you will only half
Object to this tingling reminder that nothing
Can be taken for granted. Today and always,
That snap and nerve of something prepared
To risk its rawness, and which still can jolt
With a simple kiss. And some one, no doubt,
Will get a poem out of this.

26th March 1994

If a day could create its image
In advance, today's would be
A step up from cool darkness
To a wedge of door opening
Straight to the dazzle of summer –
The tarmac's shimmering bake,
A breeze that just riffles the grasses,
All water flaring, and all
Machinery quelled to a murmur.

For you, I would want that landscape
To be as welcome as Cosdon
Glimpsed on your way home,
And quirky as the progression
Of a geographer's ABC –
From alluvial fans, to a basket
Of eggs terrain, to the chatter marks
On pebbles, past river régimes
To the zero curtain zone.

Even that rounding to silence
At the literal end, in the cold
Shadow of the heat, can become
Our invitation to follow
A writer's or traveller's instinct –
To keep on the move, and make
The map by whatever projections
Love may delight to draw
From the data of our given days.

Coming Down

In these scales, nothing
Is properly weighed –
Yet it is here
That you feel the machine
Feeling the full
Weight of its weight,
Each muscle of metal
As tested and stressed
As an old kneecap,
As the plane jags down
The staircase of air.

And for ever, until
The landing, it seems
That the land runs on
And on, below:
Lower, lower –
To the speeding cornfields,
The flicking hyphens,
Down through the airlock
Of absolutes, to the heart
With its balancing feather; to you
Waiting, on the light earth.

3

Unspoken

(for Erica)

Unsuccessful snow has been falling
Almost all day onto Scottish stone
The colour and the texture of tongue –
Flakes that race in a skirling gale
And pour across baronial turrets
Above the brown rout of the Esk.

Shortly the measures of time and distance
Will be overcome by our two voices
Piped and thin, accorded space
Between the clunk of falling coins.
Neither will say what both know.
We may discuss the gale, the unsettled snow.

Sublunary

The moon's second reflection,
As it drifts into the depths
Of summer fields and turns us
To ghosts in our own landscapes,
Is the image of its ambitions –
To send the river rattling
Off on its stones; to outstare
The crop-eared owl; to reach
Right down to the dust
Of the tight avenues of wheat
And draw out from the earth
The monthly fullness of silence.

Prelude

Something is not being said,
But waited for all the same;
A train, perhaps,
Or a revolution,
Or an unjust king with a sword.

But the rim of a halo
Is understood, the current of air
From a bright wing flexing:
And somewhere a choir
Is floating its precise dictions
Calmly, beyond the announced silence.

The Sea Again

This sea to which
I stay faithful in failure
Is dark slate now
And finely wrinkled,
The skin on the back
Of an old hand.

Close to, far —
Easing to shore
With a flick of the wrist;
In the channel, one buoy,
Peppermint green,
The miracle mitre
Of a sunken bishop;
Short of the horizon,
A wide swathe
Of palest blue.

Beyond measure
It shines from within
As if all the figures
Of lights and bearings
Could happily be taken
Into one brimming tide.

Umbrian Song

(for Jimmy and Margie Campbell)

You have come to a landscape of transformations
Where hoses project white feather after feather
Across the maize, and every sunset
Is a Japanese flag flying close alongside
The flank of a Japanese volcano.

Locked in its dull tent, the caterpillar
Changes in private: but the scorpion crossing
The whitewashed wall is caught halfway
Between its lobster imitation and being
A sleek black galley with a high prow.

The breeze and the poplar, a double act,
Exactly merge to a full river's trickle –
And even time is no more, here,
Than a single laryngitic cockerel
And random churchbells tuned to no hour.

As for the sunflowers, they droop and droop,
Field on field of blackening shower-heads...
Meanwhile you sweat and sweep and scrape
And paint like fury, stubbornly shaping
The labour of love to a real house.

Grounded

I am writing this from the Hotel Jagsons Regency.
In Nagpur, of course. I did not mean to be here.
The plane is grounded. According to the guidebook
This is the orange-growing centre of India.
All is well. There always is a voice
At the other end of the line. The fan is working.
Nagpur is on the river Nag. The management
Has thoughtfully put some matches and a candle
Out in my room, in case of a sudden power-cut.
The plane, it seems, was struck by lightning. Soon
They will send another plane, I'm sure. Perhaps
Later today. Last night, from the airport,
I managed to contact home. My daughter's voice
Was good to hear. My son, she says, is cheerful
In hospital. Someone was waiting, yesterday,
To meet me. I am sharing this hotel room
With an elderly army major. He has three children.
Luckily, my hand luggage does include
A change of underwear, clean socks and shirt.
Now it is just a matter of passing the time.
Lightning never strikes the same plane twice.
Jagsons Regency is not a usual name
For a hotel. The whirring of the fan
Could become irksome. Perhaps there will be a meal.
Later, I might go out and look at oranges.

Oxford in Winter

Exposed, the political geography of the season –
The bleak grandiloquent hard up against
That English speciality, the hunched demotic.

Dichotomies ache with self-love. Discuss. The Isis
Swills upstream on its own back, a swash
Of grey-green oilcloth: when still, is quite opaque.

The clipped box-hedges fronting the Botanic Gardens
Protect bare rose-stalks virtuously from
Condensed palms that sweat in their mini-tropics.

The High, meanwhile, has skeins of air as elastic
As Boyle and Hooke could have wished. In Christ Church Meadow
Some nervy tourists, caught by their cameras, smile.

Restaurants puff out their fug. Shops and centres
Vainly proliferate. Grimly the crowd patrols
The shining malls, their miles of touted goods.

A silhouetted cyclist, however, pedals
Slowly over Donnington Bridge, alleging the right
To dream, though the only wet in his dream is a dream.

The city as *palazzo*, its wonder half decay,
Where the lordly light flickers, almost is absorbed...
The crack you hear is the spine of the splayed book, breaking.

The Landscape of Threat

The end of surprise: or the start
Of an understatement that plays
The lower cases to advantage.
A matter of the ice, perhaps,
In the wind that swoops up to the ridge;
Or the water too cloudy to fathom
In the old ironstone quarries;
Or the light that sears like pure acid
At the rim of the rolling cloudbase.

Lost among fields, beyond
The saplings collared in tubes,
The works are long low buildings
Apparently deserted and closed.
But all of them, you are sure,
Have no end of little rooms
With darkening stains on the walls,
Windows that ward off the glare,
An atmosphere stale with questions.

Incidentals will do here: no need
For emblems. The imagination
Is a hostage to market forces,
And truth is nothing but fact.
On the road, the splayed fruit-skin
Means nothing, even if it makes you
Think of your head split wide open
On the tarmac. So why is your heart
Racing, and something telling you to run?

Fish Magic

Here lies the holy fish: its fading gloss
Comes off as tacky sequins on your hand.
Nothing averts its eyes of milk and glass,
Or improves the dead sourness
Of its downturned mouth.

White meat conveyed to the white tooth,
That melts in a memory of salt,
That leaves its last taste on your tongue –
But it leaps to life in a thousand
Chevrons of bone, is away
In infinite flicks of muscle,
In the only afterlife it knows,
The resurrection of numbers.

Pistachios and Mussels

Age by colour and in wrinkles:
The withheld, the clitoral,
The green of a vivid sapling,
The orange-grey of nothing else.

The secret that must be prised
Or bitten apart;
Analogies, if any,
By rhyme – gloss, loss:
The body, the heart.

Three Sonnets

Age to Age
(for Peter Scupham)

The last exhibit in the museum of poise is
One white cup on one white saucer, shown
Together with associated noises –
The clink of spoon, too telltale to disown;
The chink of china set down, after the trill
Of tea sucked up across the glittering rim.
Imagine it – pale, set on the grainy sill
Of dusk, the world half dream and growing dim.

The deeper bowl upon the shallower spells
A sense of balance that outdoes mere survival,
Just as the dainty but brittle handle tells
Of an elegance that somehow goes on thriving –
Even when a new age, clamorous, insists
On rights, bawling, banging down mugs and fists.

Digital Time

Officiously it flicks its one-off fractions,
The little lit-up bits of background eights,
Each blink of lapse a finely tuned exaction.
Inaudible or bleeping, never late,
It prints across the brain in shifting neon
The proof of isolation, here and now
Broken to there and then, the speeding aeons
Of all the splitting seconds time allows.

But once, coddled in a lined pocket, or strapped
To your wrist, it was the whole globe you wore,
Where present, past and future overlapped
As naturally as waves upon the shore –
And time's escapement, by simple tick and tock,
Relayed the beat of the heart to the face of the clock.

Party Game

One layer, then the next, until inside
The head as well the music stops, restarts –
And the perplexing game goes on, through pride
Or some absurd compulsion of the heart.
One layer, then another, till the air
Itself must choke on paper, and the string
Trip all the players up, before the bare
Truth can put an end to everything.

Music, silence, tearing, more music – at last
A box! The lid ripped off. Inside, one layer
Of paper, then another. Music – time to pass
The nightmare package on to the nextdoor player:
And though they fear the worst, the hope of winning
Is never quite resolved. Again, they begin.

Fireflies

Sure as nightfall, finer
Than any drizzle, their tweaks of light
Are brief, occulting – so little
You'd think they must be splinters
Of a single idea.

Out in the dusk, they almost
Are beyond the limit of what is possible
For a man or god to invent –
Are never quite where they were
And outflank order.

The grass is theirs, the woodpile,
The hedgerow, all the darkening air –
Even if you close your eyes
They are there, navigating in silence
To the sill of your dream.

Cranach's Eve

The last of innocence, you'd say
Perhaps, until you see the way
That little finger nicely stretches
Out, and that sparse foliage fetches
Up across the groin. And whose
Teethmarks have made the apple lose
Its roundness? Even without the snake
Coiling its fishy lobes, you'd make
The right deduction: innocence already
Gone. That challenging look is steady
As knowledge and as incomplete –
The globe trembles under her feet.

The Fullness of Glory

What narrative can move the silence on,
What silence appropriate the cries
Of those abandoned day after day by any
Hope of simple justice or of mercy?

It is more than our curiosity
Which betrays us. Yesterday, how peacefully
The stars shone! And any fruit, cut open,
Models the pure cosmology of perfection.

Propped on the Easter altar, the book still trails
Its markers of gold fire, imperial purple,
Dark crimson. Each week, from its spread pages,
Is read *Heaven and earth are full of Thy glory.*

The contexts accrue – another starving child
Hunching over the wreck of its own poor bones;
And, after stories censored by curt gunfire,
Accusations that hang like smoke in the silence.

Songs of the Darkness

In the buried darkness
Voices are welling
That sing and pray
In a language almost
To be understood.

In the painted darkness
The magi ride onward
With their blazing retinues,
Ignoring the huntsman
Who aches for blood.

In the darkness outside,
The leprous cities
And lush fields
Embody the world
In its broken beauty.

In songs of the darkness
The flowers of the dead
Are always in bloom,
And the birth of Christ
Is God's first wound.

Yet out of the darkness
Come such simple offerings
As ghee, fou-fou
Or maize, gifts made kingly
By the recognition of love.

A Christmas Candle

It begins as a crackling star
On the soft flesh of tallow,
Draws up to a little arch,
Burrows a molten pool
Tremulous as a tear.

And this recurs, where before
There was only a dull stump,
An opaque pronoun; where the snuff,
Black, curled over above
The rim, hung there merely.

Vowel of Christ and child,
Its bodied brightness invests
The dark with wild shadows,
The old conspiracies
That hope must still compile.

Though time will bring it down,
It accepts the alighting flame;
Though in the night-time draughts
It gutters and sweals, yet
Fiercely it burns. Again. Now.

The Open Door

(for Jill Balcon)

Just beyond the threshold
Wallflowers load the air
With sexy smells, while the fountain
Creates diversions, drawing
Its dotted fleur-de-lys
Again and again.

Having escaped the house-lime –
Its tender baffles, its veins
Like systems of worry – a single
Strip of sunlight stretches
Out on the dark coolness
Of the stone floor.

And the door as it is, open,
Is neither an invitation
Nor a direction – only,
As the room is, and the garden,
Unblurred, perennial, going
Nowhere but here.

Wallace Stevens at Hawthornden

Each walk around the castle brings
Its repeated challenge – how to catch
The pheasant's unspeakable cry in words,
A single word that fairly prints
The monosyllable that you hear.

He'll have you at it day and night,
Inventing words that won't quite do,
Any of them, even if some
Might be components, or cognate with
The monosyllable that you hear.

While *Chorp* and *Cronk* might qualify
So, too, would *Cark* – or should it be
Chowk or *Trark*, *Thrak* or *Thronk?*
Each one of these records in part
The monosyllable that you hear.

But what might seem supremely best
Is still an approximate fiction, needing
The rasp of clutch-plates and of rust,
A chreotechnical echo, to be
The monosyllable that you hear.

The pheasant knows the poet's aim –
Exploding from the undergrowth
He'll keep him questing for precision,
But humble too: the single cry
The poet hears is, simply, *Try*.

Father to Son

(for Matthew)

No one would know, unless they actually knew –
Or even notice the drab brown building facing
The Apollo supermarket. Once inside,
Traffic noise or the odd branch waving from
Beyond the window are insufficient distractions
From evidence which multiplies in folders,
Time that aches and aches in clinic queues
And the outraged screams of children.

Each time we go, my heart begins to sink
Almost as much as yours must – most of all
When we first glimpse, beyond a door, then confront
Those alien machines, grotesque or sleek,
Whose circuits you, their missing part, must complete.
With all their tubes, dials, monitors and screens,
We have to trust them as benign, despite
The pain they may also bring.

Beyond all this – the caring smiles and skills
Of nurses and radiographers, and the doctors
So famous that, jet-lagged, they have to ring
In from the airport to give the go-ahead
For pre-meds; beyond the knowledge, too, that others
Are suffering more – a part of you still craves
A chance to reject it all.

And part of me, confounded by love and fear,
Would almost sign a pact as your accomplice –
Anything rather than more tinkering to cope
With a defect no one can help. Almost – forgive
That qualifying doubt whose other side
Is hope. Beyond a certain point of bruising
Neither can talk of this.

The Sitting-Room

(in memory of Alan Hancox, bookseller)

Something was always veiled,
Like pride, in that buckskin light
Where chairs staged their colloquies –
Something that gave the air
Its grain, but knew how warmth
Could master the edge of wit,
Though never blunt it: a kindness
Kept between stout boards.

And the books – imagine them now
Lying open, their spines
Arched, mild revelations
Of a life simply to be read:
Their pages that flick through silence
And hold good as a true colophon.

Fanfares at Eger

They appear on the hour, like figures
Geared to an antique clock,
Pinned on the narrow balcony
Of the town's thin minaret –
So high that you cannot make out
Their features, only admire
The last of the sunlight gleaming
On the bell of the wound horn,
The great golden paperclip
Of the trombone's slide, the valves
Of the two brilliant trumpets.

For half an hour exactly
They drive the birds crazy
With their rich party pieces –
Black as quavers, the swallows
Race through the pressured air,
Criss-crossing the flourishes,
The fanfares and the canzonas.
And, down below, a circle
Of pale faces peering, smiling;
And, inch by inch, the light going.

It could not reach out far,
This music, will never alight on
The still, green valley of Lídice,
Will not infiltrate
The huge, strutting concrete
Of Bucharest's leaky palace –
Yet even though, long ago,
The players bowed, turned and
Disappeared, the echo goes on.

Lawrence Sail was born in London in 1942 and brought up in the West Country. A freelance writer, he has published seven collections of poems, most recently *Out of Land: New & Selected Poems* (1992) and *Building into Air* (1995), both from Bloodaxe. His poems have been broadcast on radio and television, and he has presented *Poetry Now* (BBC Radio 3) and *Time for Verse* (BBC Radio 4). A former editor of *South West Review* (from 1981 to 1985), he has also compiled several anthologies, including *First and Always* (Faber, 1988). He reviews for *PN Review*, *Poetry Review* and *Stand*.

He was chairman of the Arvon Foundation from 1990 to 1994. In 1991 he was programme director of the Cheltenham Festival of Literature, and a Whitbread Book of the Year Judge. He was awarded a Hawthornden Fellowship in 1992, and an Arts Council Writer's Bursary in 1993. In the same year he undertook a month-long tour of India for the British Council. In 1994 he was the British jury member for the European Literature Prize.